412857

D1760159

PIC NIC

POP-FOLK CONTEMPORARY ILLUSTRATION
ILLUSTRATION POP-FOLK CONTEMPORAINE
ILUSTRACIÓN POP-FOLK CONTEMPORÁNEA

RETINA & RETINETTE

promopress

PICNIC

Pop-Folk Contemporary Illustration
Illustration Pop-Folk Contemporaine
Ilustración Pop-Folk Contemporánea

ISBN: 978-84-92810-17-8
© 2011 PROMOPRESS
© 2011 Retina y Retinette

Promopress is a commercial brand of:
Promotora de prensa internacional SA
c/ Ausias march 124
08013 Barcelona (Spain)
T: (+34) 93 245 14 64 F: (+34) 93 265 48 93
mail: info@promopress.es
www.promopress.info

Idea: Juan Cardosa y Júlia Solans. Retina y Retinette.
Dirección de arte: Juan Cardosa
Diseño y maquetación: Retina y Retinette
Portada: Júlia Solans
Prólogo: Conxita Fornieles
Fotografía: Roser Solans
Textos, edición y traducción: Satèl·lit bcn + Hugo Steckelmacher y Olivier Gilbert
Imprime: Toppan Leefung
Primera edición: 2011

Printed in China

CONTENTS

-

What is the idea behind *Picnic*?

// The best way to answer that question is with a list of some of our favourite things from the world of illustration: the golden age of the 1960s and 70s in Europe and the US, Polish poster art, the cartoons or "animated caricatures" of John Hubley (Mr. Magoo) and Friz Freleng (The Pink Panther), the advent of "Pop Art" courtesy of graphic artists such as Heinz Edelman, Milton Glaser and Paul Rand, the Tiki style that landed on our shores via the Pacific, among others. The aim of *Picnic* is to bring together all of these influences in which craftsmanship, low costs, collage, a fusion of techniques, chance and texture all have a vital role. All of this on top of the book's main conceptual crux – a devotion to synthesis –with the result a series of genuine visual poems, masterpieces of new visual communication. We sought to create a piece (in the form of a book) that, beyond merely being inspirational, would be the sort that you take to bed with you, where you can delight in each author's illustrations, letting your imagination run wild and filling your sleep with dreams.

Do your mothers know this is what you do for a living?

// Actually, they think we've graduated and paid off our mortgages. They also think we did an MBA at Harvard and that they have the most handsome grandchildren on earth. And they believe this hobby of ours is really great...
(P.S.: we send our mothers our love)

Do you have any advice for illustrators who are just starting out?

// We believe it is important to encourage the art of observation. When you study an illustration, there's a whole process you have to go through in order to approach it properly. First, displaying curiosity, you pick out the bit that you like the most (be it the paper, the colours or the texture). Then, if you can, and providing there's no one watching, you touch the paper on which it is drawn (or else, printed) and, lastly, smell it. Now is the time to carry out a thorough analysis of the techniques employed by the illustrator or artist. The next step is to go home. Give your eyes a break. And then simply start going through reams of paper until you find your own style. Just as the process began with observation, so it ends with it, as those coming up behind you embark on the very same process you did when you were just starting out.

What does the future hold for the industry?

// Industries that revolve around creativity and invention are by nature infinite and endless. We believe that *Picnic* demonstrates that illustration is currently one of the most popular areas within graphic, artistic and business circles, a vital tool with countless professional applications related to the world of advertising, design and fashion. Illustration has shown itself to be fully up to the task of adapting, evolving and riding the wave of possibilities offered by new digital tools.

Do you think the illustration fad is bound to pass?

// At present, much use is being made of illustration in design. We believe there are two basic reasons for this: firstly, we are living in an age where pleasant, accessible images are being drawn on extensively.
On the other hand, there has been a vast proliferation of illustrators, owing to some extent both to the increased ability to show off your portfolio (via the internet), and also to the fact that illustration is no longer considered the preserve of journalistic caricatures and political cartoons.
Illustration continues to gain momentum and take shape with each passing day. Plus, without meaning to sound pretentious, all fashions had to be sketched by someone first.

If you hadn't become illustrators, what would you have liked to be?

// In all likelihood we'd have ended up being two fairytale characters and been rejected by Disney.

How did you go about choosing what to include in the book?

// There is an abundance of talent out there on the internet. Through Flickr, blogs and other websites we built up a pool of illustrators who showed off their work. Some of this work was flawless, and a large amount of it went on to occupy the pages of this *Picnic*. We believed that in order for the book to accurately reflect the current landscape of the illustration scene, it was important to scour the internet in order to uncover these new talents, who so openly and generously display their work online. We are diehard fans of the internet, and all the more so due to the industry we work in. The world of pixels is a vast window, a shop window even, where you can find anything you're looking for. And this feeling of amazement before and admiration for unknown talent from all over the world was the inspiration behind *Picnic*.

And, lastly, what would you never forget to take with you on a picnic?

// A red-and-white chequered table cloth, pickles, serviettes, mosquito repellent, sunglasses, ice, toothpicks, a thermos full of coffee, trees and ants, a little wicker basket, glasses, a freshly baked baguette, pink champagne, homemade brownies, and a cushion and a blanket so we can take a nap. Oooh, loads of things.

D'où vient *Picnic* ?

// Nous allons énumérer une série d'éléments du monde de l'illustration qui nous a émue : l'âge d'or des années 60 et 70 en Amérique du Nord et en Europe, l'affiche polonaise, les dessins animés ou les « caricatures animées » de John Hubley (Mister Magoo) et Friz Freleng (La Panthère Rose), l'avènement du pop art sous l'impulsion de designers tels que Heinz Edelmann, Milton Glaser et Paul Rand, le style tiki originaire du Pacifique, etc. *Picnic* a pour but de réunir toutes ces merveilleuses influences où la main, le faible coût, le collage, le mélange des techniques, le hasard et la texture sont primordiaux. Tout cela renforcé par son profond contenu conceptuel, cette synthèse livre de véritables poèmes visuels, chefs-d'œuvre de la communication visuelle. Nous avons voulu créer une pièce (sous forme de livre) qui pourrait non seulement être source d'inspiration, mais aussi un livre à feuilleter au lit et ainsi prendre plaisir à chaque image en inventant des contes et des histoires pour s'endormir et rêver intensément.

Vos mères savent que vous vous consacrez à ce sujet?

// En fait, elles croient que nous avons terminé nos études et que nous avons remboursé notre crédit immobilier. Elles pensent aussi que nous avons fait un MBA à Harvard et que leurs petits-enfants sont les plus mignons sur terre. Et notre passe-temps leur semble très agréable...
(PS: un baiser à nos mères)

Un conseil pour les tous nouveaux illustrateurs

// Nous croyons qu'il faut encourager l'art de l'observation. Lorsque vous avez une illustration en face de vous, vous devez suivre un processus pour vous en approcher : vous devez le faire avec curiosité, en vous interrogeant sur les détails qui vous plaisent le plus (est-ce le papier, la couleur, la texture ?) puis, si vous le pouvez et à condition que personne ne vous surveille, vient le toucher du papier sur lequel elle est dessinée (ou imprimée) et enfin la perception olfactive de l'illustration. Ensuite examinez en détail la technique utilisée par l'illustrateur ou l'artiste. L'étape suivante est de rentrer chez vous, reposer vos yeux et commencer à griffonner sur papier vos idées pour trouver votre propre style. L'observation est le début mais aussi la fin lorsque ceux qui viennent après vous utilisent le même processus que vous aviez initialisé.

Comment voyez-vous l'avenir de la profession?

// Les professions qui gravitent autour de la créativité et de la création sont, par nature infinies et sans fin. Nous pensons que *Picnic* montre aujourd'hui que l'illustration est une des disciplines les plus en vogue dans le monde graphique, artistique et des affaires ainsi qu'un outil essentiel pour de nombreuses applications professionnelles liées aux secteurs de la publicité, du design et de la mode. L'illustration a été en mesure de s'adapter, d'évoluer et d'exploiter les avantages que fournissent les outils numériques.

Pensez-vous que la fièvre et la mode de l'illustration tomberont en désuétude?

// Dans le panorama actuel, l'illustration est utilisée dans le design, et ceci, nous croyons, pour deux raisons fondamentales. D'une part, nous sommes dans une époque qui utilise des images séduisantes et accessibles. D'autre part et d'une certaine façon, on a assisté à une prolifération des illustrateurs entretenue par la possibilité de présenter leurs portfolios (à travers Internet) et aussi parce que l'illustration n'est plus seulement cantonnée dans la bande dessinée caricaturale et le dessin satirique dans la presse. Chaque jour, l'illustration prend forme et continue à gagner du terrain. En outre, sans vouloir être prétentieux, toute mode a été dans un premier temps dessinée par quelqu'un.

Si vous n'aviez pas été illustrateur, qu'auriez vous aimé être?

// Très probablement nous serions nés comme deux personnages de contes pour enfants, mais très certainement, Disney ne nous aurait pas embauché.

Quel fut le processus de sélection?

// Internet fourmille de talents. Grâce aux comptes Flickr, blogs et sites web, nous avons rencontré un grand nombre d'illustrateurs qui montraient leur travail. Certains de ces travaux étaient irréprochables, et un grand nombre d'entre eux figurent aujourd'hui dans les pages de *Picnic*. Nous avons estimé que pour faire un livre qui dépeint le panorama de l'illustration, nous devions enquêter sur Internet et découvrir ces nouveaux talents qui exposent ouvertement et généreusement leurs travaux. Nous sommes de grands fans du web, en particulier lorsque nous nous sommes engagés dans cette profession. Le monde du pixel est une grande fenêtre et aussi une vitrine où vous pouvez trouver tout ce que vous voulez. Ainsi est né *Picnic*, de la surprise et de l'engouement pour le talent inconnu et international.

Et pour terminer, qu'est-ce que vous n'oublierez jamais pour un pique-nique ?

// Un tissu à carreaux rouge et blanc, des cornichons, des serviettes de table, un anti-moustique, des lunettes de soleil, des glaçons, des cure-dents, un thermos de café, des arbres et des fourmis, un panier en osier, des verres, une baguette de pain fraîchement sortie du four, un champagne rosé, des brownies faits maison, un coussin pour faire la sieste et une couverture. Oh! Beaucoup de choses.

¿De dónde nace *Picnic*?

// Vamos a enumerar una serie de cosas del mundo de la ilustración que nos emocionan: la época dorada que tuvo lugar en las décadas de los 60 y 70 del s. XX en Norteamérica y Europa, el cartelismo polaco, el cartoon o caricaturas animadas de John Hubley (El Señor Magoo) o Friz Freleng (La Pantera Rosa), el pop, de la mano de grafistas como Heinz Edelmann, Milton Glaser y Paul Rand, el estilo tiki procedente del Pacífico, etc. *Picnic* pretende unir todas estas influencias maravillosas donde la mano, el low cost, el collage, el mestizaje de técnicas, el accidente y la textura son fundamentales. Todo ello sumado a su gran carga conceptual, la síntesis, da como resultado verdaderos poemas visuales, obras maestras de la nueva comunicación visual.

Queríamos crear una pieza (en forma de libro) que pudiera no solo ser inspiradora, sino también un libro para llevarse a la cama y recrearse en cada ilustración a fin de inventarse cuentos e historias para ir a dormir y soñar mucho.

¿Vuestras madres saben que os dedicáis a esto?

// En realidad, ellas creen que terminamos nuestros estudios y que hemos acabado de pagar la hipoteca. También piensan que hicimos un MBA en Harvard y que sus nietos son los más guapos de la tierra. Y este hobby que tenemos les parece muy bonito...
(PD: Mandamos un beso a nuestras madres)

Algún consejo para ilustradores primerizos.

// Creemos que hay que fomentar el arte de la observación. Cuando tienes una ilustración delante de ti, tienes que seguir un procedimiento para acercarte a ella: debes hacerlo con curiosidad, ponderar qué detalle te gusta más (¿es el papel, el color, la textura?) y, si es posible y no hay nadie vigilando, tocar el papel sobre el cual está dibujada (o, en su defecto, impresa) y, finalmente, olerla. Luego examina en profundidad la técnica que ha usado el ilustrador o artista. El siguiente paso es llegar a casa, relajar la vista y empezar a gastar papel hasta encontrar tu propio estilo. La observación es el principio, pero será el fin cuando aquellos que vienen por detrás de ti hagan lo mismo que tú hiciste cuando comenzaste.

¿Cómo veis el futuro del oficio?

// Las profesiones que giran en torno a la creatividad y la creación son de por sí infinitas e interminables. Creemos que *Picnic* demuestra que hoy en día la ilustración es una de las disciplinas más en boga dentro de los ámbitos gráfico, artístico y empresarial así como una herramienta fundamental en infinidad de aplicaciones profesionales ligadas al mundo de la publicidad, el diseño y la moda. La ilustración ha sabido adaptarse, evolucionar y subirse al carro de la facilidad que brindan las herramientas digitales.

¿Creéis que pasará la fiebre y la moda de la ilustración?

/ /En el panorama actual, el diseño está echando mucha mano de la ilustración, creemos que por dos motivos fundamentales: en primer lugar, estamos en un tiempo que recurre a imágenes amables y cercanas; por otra parte, ha habido una gran proliferación de ilustradores, en cierto modo, gracias a la posibilidad de mostrar sus porfolios (entiéndase Internet) y también porque la ilustración ha dejado de usarse meramente dentro del espacio reservado a la viñeta caricaturesca y la crítica en la prensa. La ilustración cobra peso y cuerpo día a día. Además, y sin querer ser pretenciosos, todas las modas las ha dibujado alguien.

Si no hicieseis lo que hacéis, ¿qué os gustaría ser?

// Muy probablemente hubiéramos nacido siendo dos personajes de cuento infantil, pero seguramente Disney no nos hubiera contratado.

¿Cómo fue el proceso de selección?

// Internet rebosa de talento. A través de cuentas de Flickr, blogs y páginas webs fuimos encontrando un montón de ilustradores que mostraban su trabajo. Algunos de estos trabajos eran impecables, y muchos de ellos llenan ahora las páginas de *Picnic*. Nos parecía que, para hacer un libro que retratase el panorama actual de la ilustración, teníamos que indagar en Internet y descubrir estos nuevos talentos que exponen su trabajo de manera abierta y generosa. Somos unos fans absolutos de la Red, sobre todo al dedicarnos a esta profesión. El mundo del píxel es una gran ventana y también un escaparate donde puedes encontrar todo lo que buscas. Así nació *Picnic*, de la sorpresa y el enamoramiento por el talento desconocido e internacional.

Y para acabar, ¿qué es lo que no olvidaríais nunca si fuerais de picnic?

// Mantel de cuadros rojos y blancos, pepinillos, servilletas, repelente contra los mosquitos, gafas de sol, hielo, palillos, termo de café, árboles y hormigas, cestito de mimbre, vasos, una baguette recién horneada, champán rosa, brownies caseros, un cojín y una manta para hacer la siesta. ¡Uf! Un montón de cosas.

//Nate Williams// *Untitled. Personal work. 2008*

//Nate Williams// *Untitled. Gööo magazine. 2009*

//**Nate Williams**// *Untitled. Personal work. 2007 (right)*
//**Nate Williams**// *Untitled. Personal work. 2009 (left)*

//**Nate Williams**// *Reading Rocket. Janus Mutual Funds. 2008*

//**Nate Williams**// *Berlin. City of Berlin. 2008*
//**Nate Williams**// *Plants hope. Ecojot. 2009*
//**Nate Williams**// *Beautiful Life. Personal work. 2009*

016

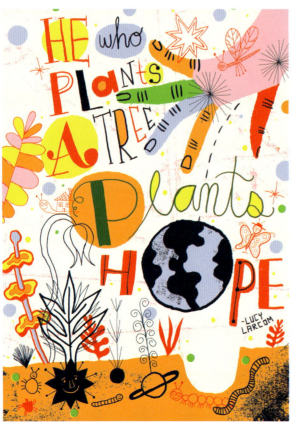

//**Nate Williams**// *Untitled. Urban out Fitters. 2008*

//Linzie Hunter// *Sometimes you just know. Art Bureau. -*

//Linzie Hunter// *Alphabet. Personal work.* -

//Linzie Hunter// *Images from Secret Weapon Spam Postcard Book. Chronicle Books. -*

//Linzie Hunter// *Images from Secret Weapon Spam Postcard Book. Chronicle Books. -*

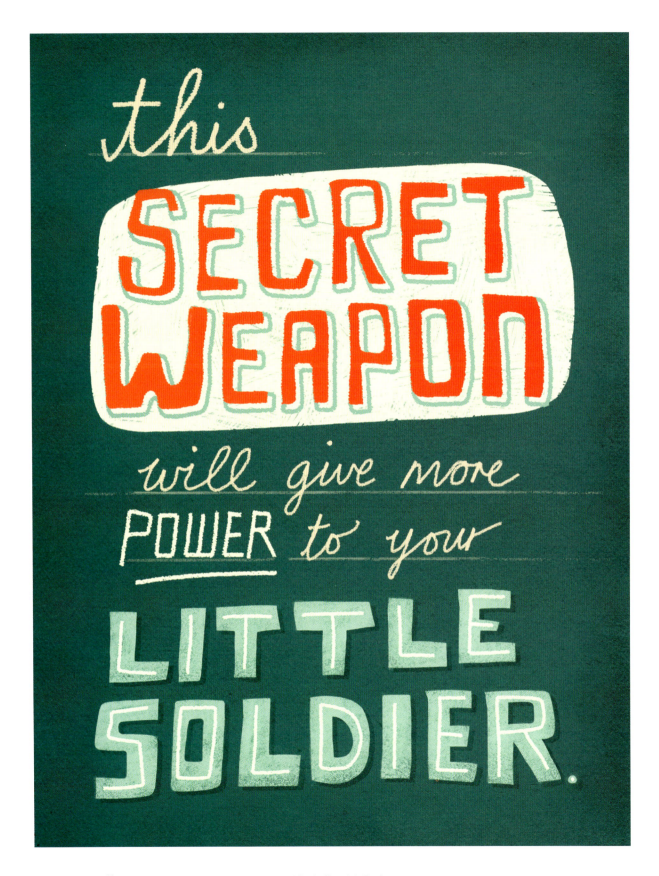

//Linzie Hunter// *Images from Secret Weapon Spam Postcard Book. Chronicle Books.* -

DON'T
PUT OFF
YOUR
HAPPY
LIFE

//Linzie Hunter// *Images from Secret Weapon Spam Postcard Book. Chronicle Books.* -

//Linzie Hunter// *Images from Secret Weapon Spam Postcard Book. Chronicle Books.* -

//Linzie Hunter// *Images from Secret Weapon Spam Postcard Book. Chronicle Books. -*

//ED// Untitled. Personal work. -

//ED// *Make me happy. Amnesty International Mexico. -*

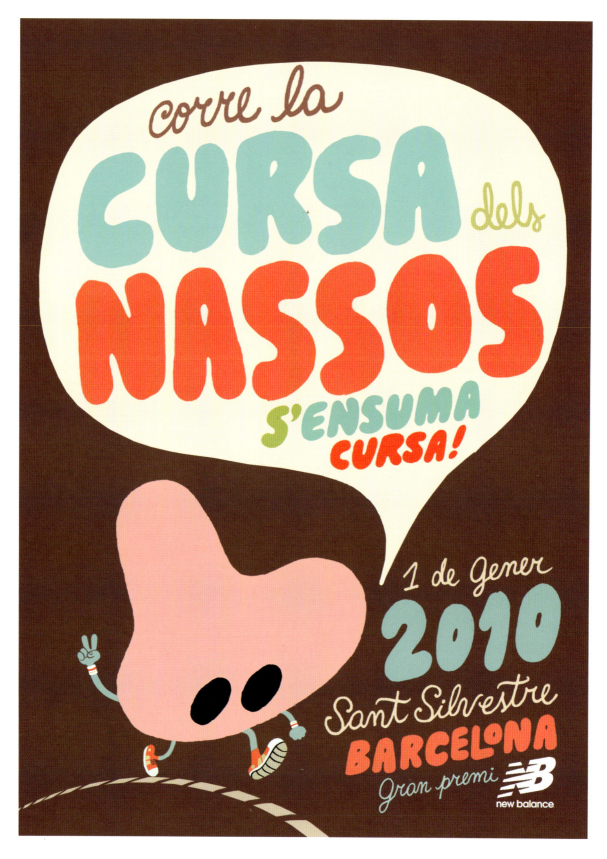

//ED// *Cursa dels nassos. New Balance.* -

//ED// *The Big One. Personal work.* -

//**Marcus Walters**// *Circle. Personal work. -*

//Marcus Walters// *Untitled. Firtrade Foundation.* -

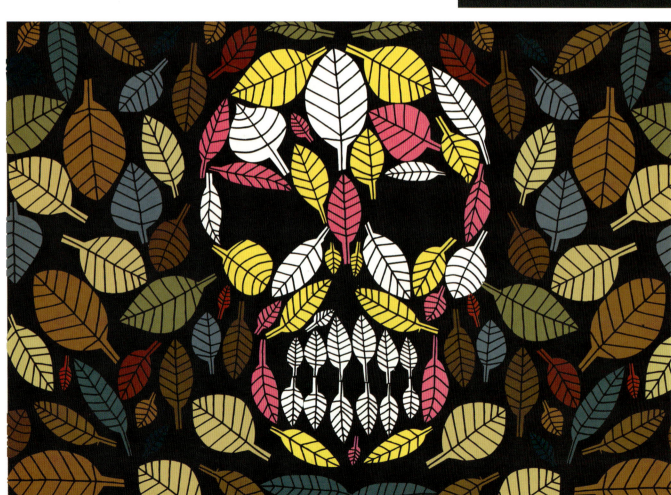

//**Marcus Walters**// *Untitled. Firtrade Foundation. -*
//**Marcus Walters**// *Skull. Personal Work. -*

//Marcus Walters// *Untitled. Monocle Magazine.* -

//**Sergio Membrillas**// *Listening to Bon Iver. Slaughterhouse Editions. 2010*
//**Sergio Membrillas**// *School. Personal work. 2009*

//Sergio Membrillas// *Rollei. Personal work. 2009*

//**Sergio Membrillas**// *Machado. Arg!. 2010 (Top)*
//**Sergio Membrillas**// *Friends. Serie Forest. 2009*
//**Sergio Membrillas**// *Bird Family. Serie Forest. 2009*

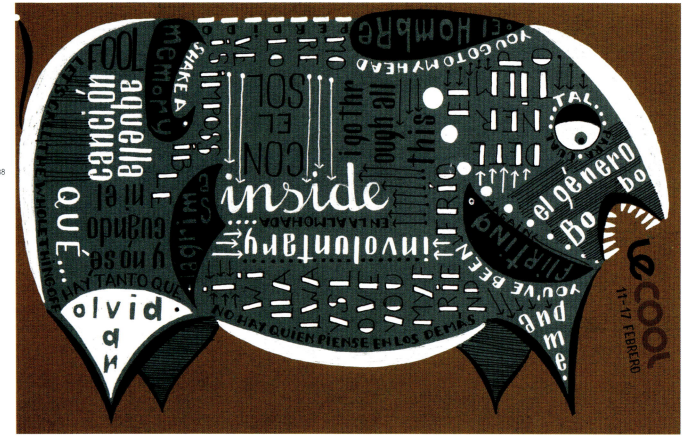

//Coqué Azcona// *Inside. Le Cool Barcelona. -*

//Coqué Azcona// *Fools Lament. Personal work.* -

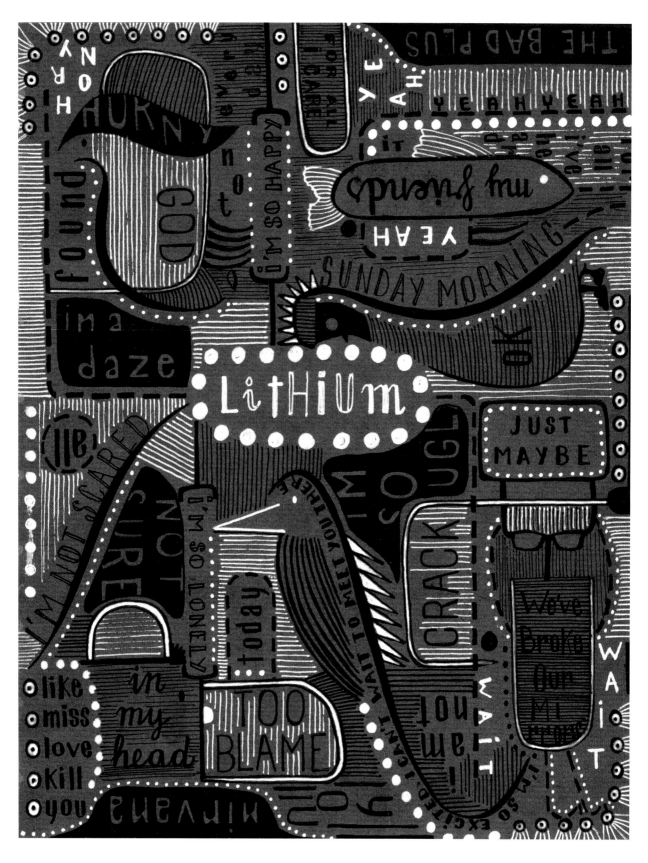

//**Coqué Azcona**// *Lithium. Personal project. -*

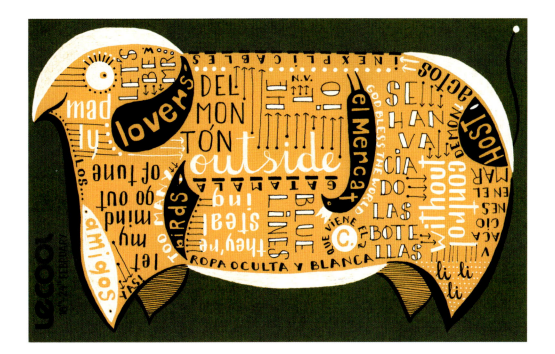

//**Coqué Azcona**// *Outside. Le Cool Barcelona.* -
//**Coqué Azcona**// *So I Threw a Bottle. Personal work.* -

//Coqué Azcona// *Money. Personal project.* -

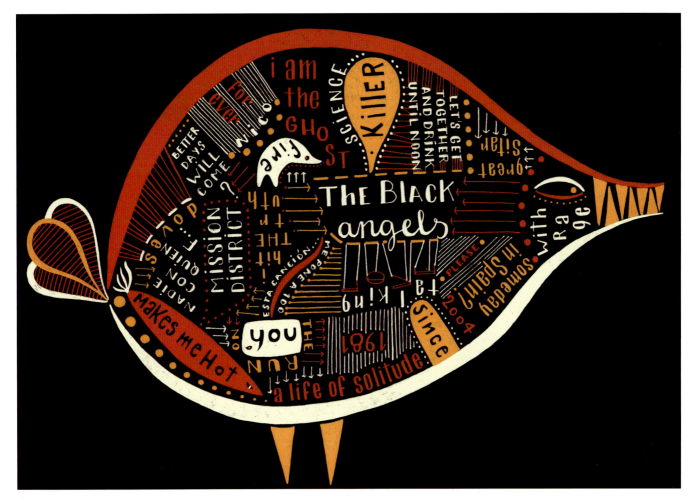

//**Coqué Azcona**// *No Drone. Personal project. -*

//**Harsapati**// *Untitled. Roja series. 2009*

//**Harsapati**// *Untitled. Personal Work. 2009*

//Harsapati// *Untitled. Roja series. 2009*

//Harsapati// *Untitled. Personal Work. 2010*
//Harsapati// *Untitled. Roja series. 2009*

//Harsapati// *Untitled. Personal Work. 2010*

//Harsapati// *Untitled. Personal Work. 2009*

//Nacho Tatjer// *Es-candy-nabo. Visual poetry book. 2010*

//**Nacho Tatjer**// *Mops. Children's Book by Eva Linsdström. 2009*

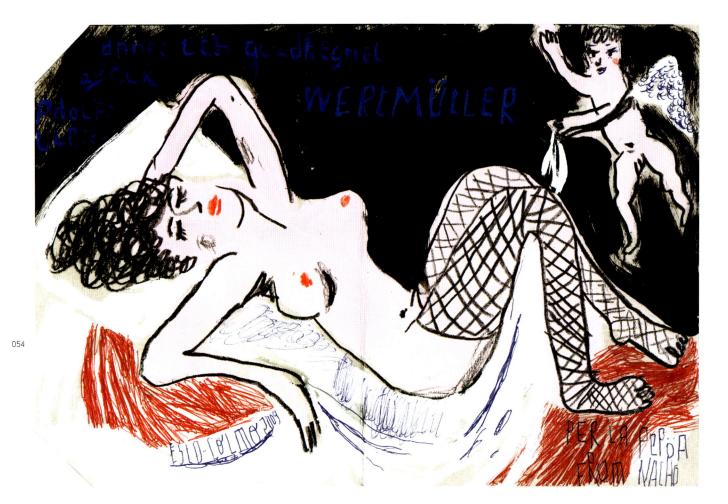

//Nacho Tatjer// *Es-candy-nabo. Visual poetry book. 2010*
//Nacho Tatjer// *Es-candy-nabo. Visual poetry book. 2010*

//Nacho Tatjer// *Pino y la bande del Pepino. Personal work. 2009*

//Marc Vicens// *Apuntes del TGV. Girona magazine. 2009*

//**Marc Vicens**// *BCN Negra. Qué Leer magazine. 2007*

//**Marc Vicens**// *Ictineu. University of Girona. 2010*
//**Marc Vicens**// *Apunts d'art. Girona magazine. 2009*

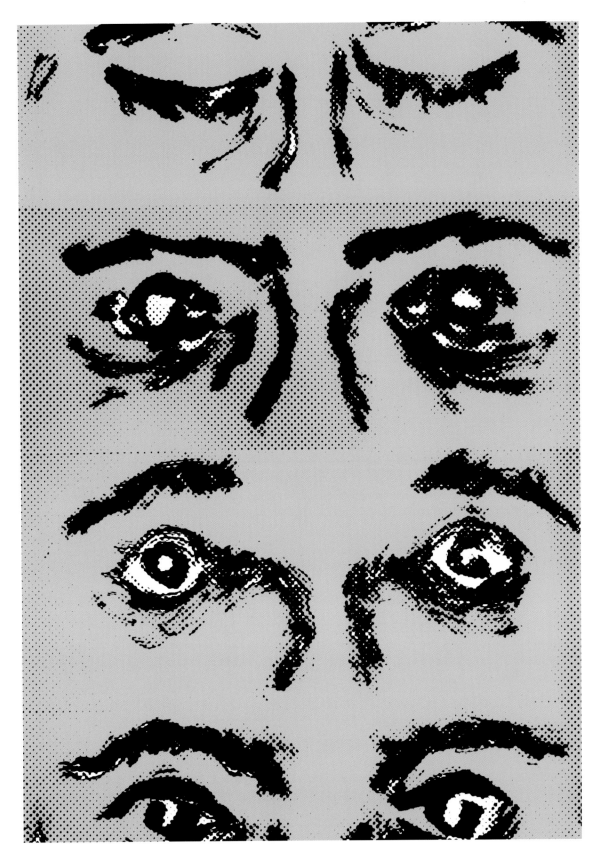

//**Marc Vicens**// *El vigilant en el camp de sègol. Engega magazine. 2009*

//Seniorita Polyester// *Roller Monkey. Personal work. 2009*

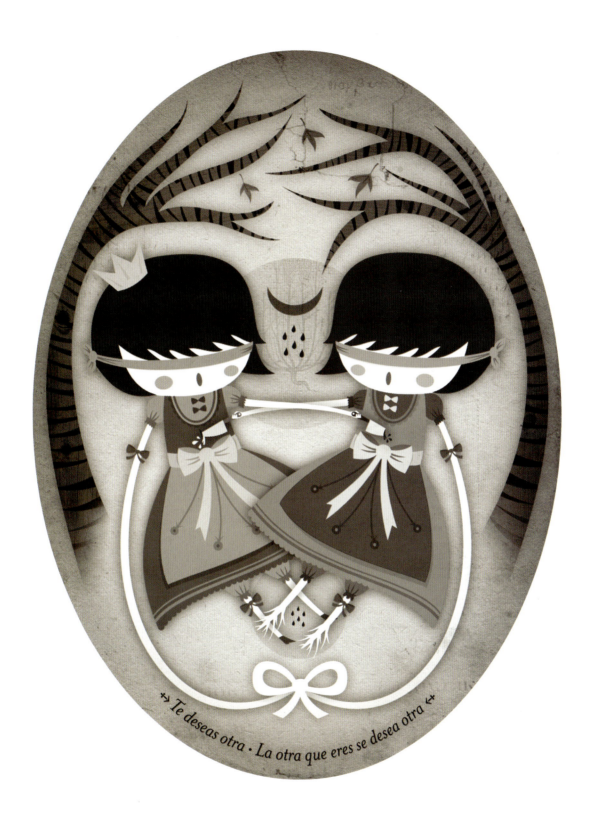

//Seniorita Polyester// *Te deseas otra. Frankenstein essays. 2008*

//Seniorita Polyester// *Petites. Petites Magazine. 2008*

//Seniorita Polyester// *Sorry Zorrito. Personal work. 2009*
//Seniorita Polyester// *Terror. Cualquier Verdura. 2009*

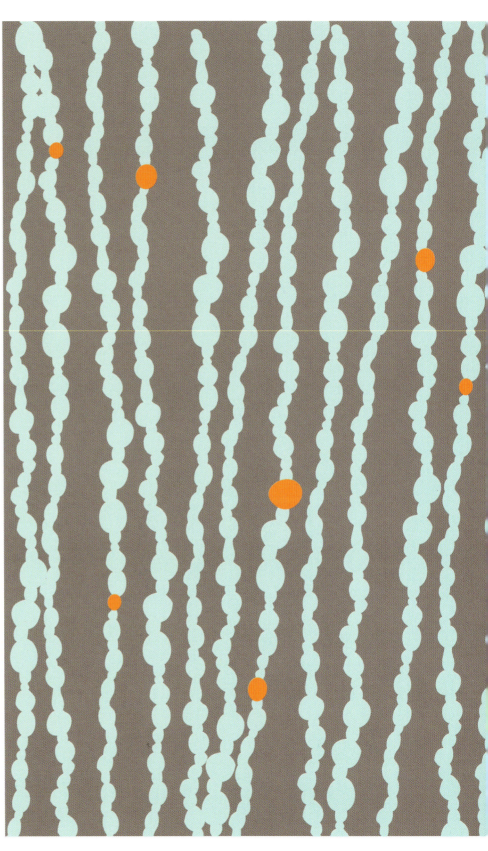

www.tadcarpenter.com

55/100

//**Tad Carpenter**// *Bird Posse. Personal work. 2010*
//**Tad Carpenter**// *Sunrise greeting card. Sunrise greeting. 2009*

//**Tad Carpenter**// *Space DJ. Aiga. 2010*

//Tad Carpenter// *Rock The Earth. Rock The Earth. 2010*

//**Tad Carpenter**// *Totem Pole. Personal work. 2009*
//**Tad Carpenter**// *Beep, Beep Bike. Cabaret poster. 2010*

//Tad Carpenter// *Sunrise greeting card. Sunrise greeting. 2009*

//Tad Carpenter// *Sunrise greeting card. Sunrise greeting. 2009*

//Pepa Prieto// *Play Be. H. Bodies. -*

//Pepa Prieto// *Untitled. Iguapop Gallery. 2009*

//Pepa Prieto// *Life is a game. Iguapop Gallery. 2009*

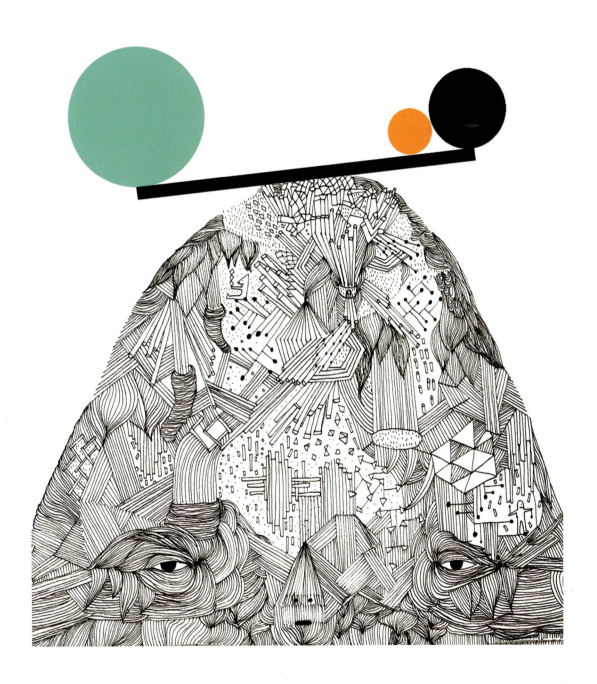

//Pepa Prieto// *Untitled. Iguapop Gallery. 2009*

//Kirstie Edmunds// *Heels. Personal work. 2009*

//Kirstie Edmunds// *Measuring Meercats. Personal work. 2009*

//Kirstie Edmunds// *Winter. Christmas card. 2009*
//Kirstie Edmunds// *Stella in the rain. Personal work. 2009*

//**Kirstie Edmunds**// *Champagne Bear. Personal work. 2009*

//Kirstie Edmunds// *Monkeys. Personal work. 2009*

//**Kirstie Edmunds**// *Monsters. Personal work. 2009*
//**Kirstie Edmunds**// *Red Riding. Personal work. 2009*

//Gustavo Aimar// *Paisaje. Personal Work. 2009*

//**Gustavo Aimar**// *La Pipa. Dossier Editions. 2009*

//Gustavo Aimar// *Cicatrices. Calibroscópio Editions. 2009*

//Gustavo Aimar// *Cicatrices 2. Calibroscópio Editions. 2009*

//Gustavo Aimar// *La Lluvia y el Sapo. Personal work. 2009*

//**Gustavo Aimar**// *Después de la lluvia. Personal work. 2009*

//Julia Pott// *Zookimono. Zookimono.* –

//Julia Pott// *Whale Hill. Proof Gallery. 2010*
//Julia Pott// *Cat and dog. Casiotone for the painfully alone. -*

 //Julia Pott// *Decemberist Still. The Decemberist. -*

RUFUS FOX

//Julia Pott// *Night Time Bear. Small Magazine. 2009*
//Julia Pott// *Wooly-Bear. Small Magazine. 2009*
//Julia Pott// *Rufus Fox. Spokesfox. -*

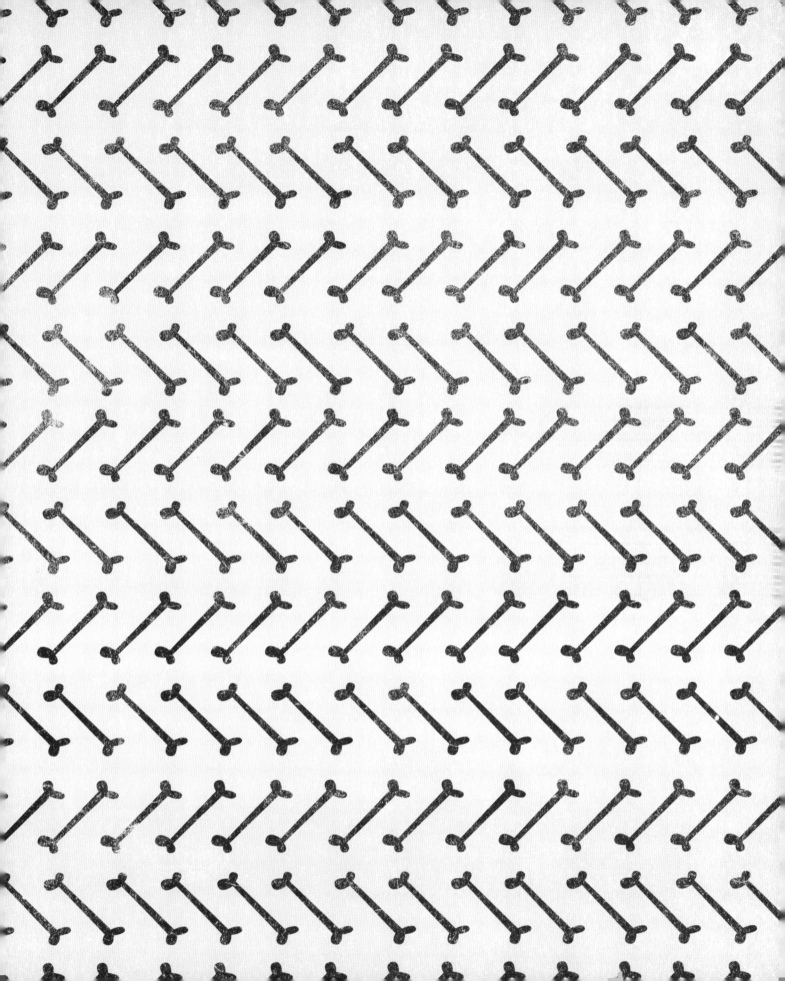

//Robert Samuel Hanson// *Untitled. Early Griffin Press. -*

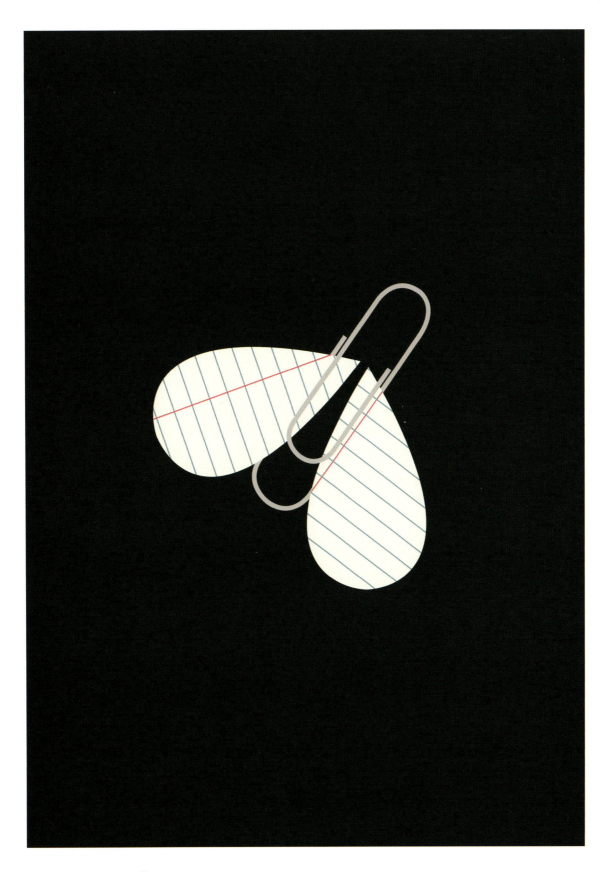

//Robert Samuel Hanson// *Untitled. Personal work. -*

//**Robert Samuel Hanson**// *Untitled. University of Toronto Magazine.* -

//Robert Samuel Hanson// *Untitled. Form Fifty Five.* -

//Robert Samuel Hanson// *Untitled. Tiny Showcase.* -

//Robert Samuel Hanson// *Untitled. Personal work.* -

//Robert Samuel Hanson// *Untitled. Monocle's Mexico, Survey supplement.* -

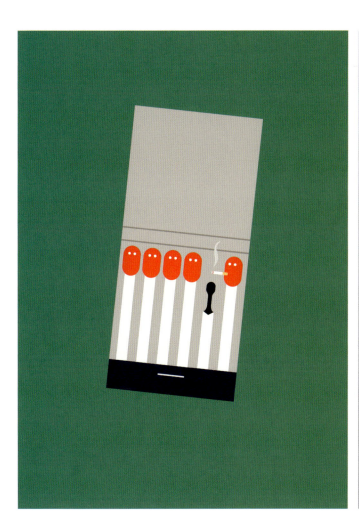

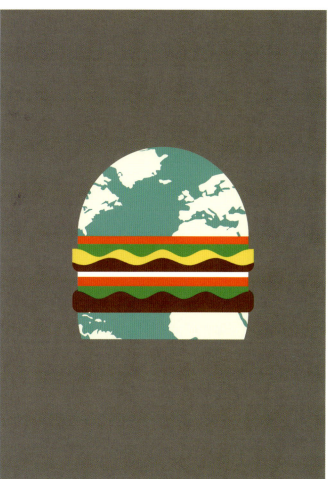

//Robert Samuel Hanson// *Untitled. Personal work.* -
//Robert Samuel Hanson// *Untitled. Personal work.* -

1.3. a

2.7.

5.1. a

1.

2.4. c

1.8. b

3.3.

4.

A4

A3

//Lotta Nieminen// *Untitled. Painomaailma magazine. -*

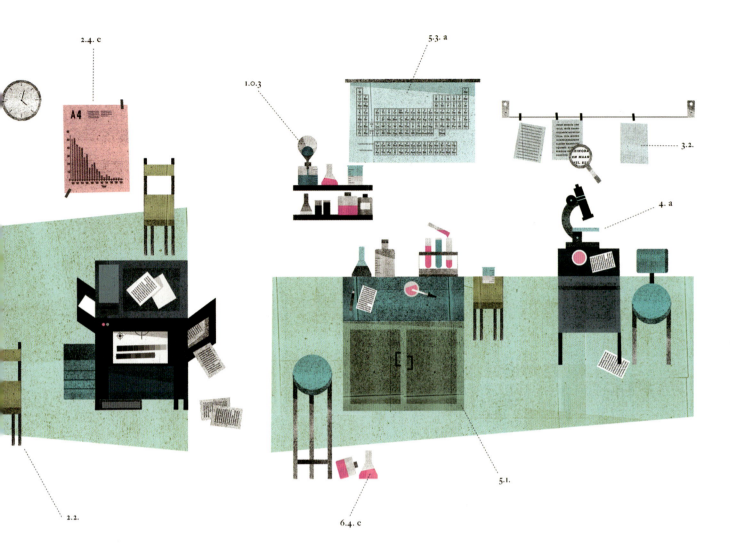

//Lotta Nieminen// *Untitled. Painomaailma magazine.* -

//Lotta Nieminen// *Untitled. Personal work.* -

//Lotta Nieminen// *Untitled. Uponor.* –

//**Lotta Nieminen**// *Untitled. Habitare. -*

//**Lotta Nieminen**// *Untitled. Aviisori magazine.* -

//Andreas Samuelsson// *Orange. Personal work.* -

//Andreas Samuelsson// *Trash. Arkitip. -*

//Andreas Samuelsson// *Kit 02. Print. -*

//Andreas Samuelsson// *Choose. Print. -*

//**Andreas Samuelsson**// *Untitled. Anorak magazine. -*

//Andreas Samuelsson// *Untitled. Personal work.* -

//**Andreas Samuelsson**// *Untitled. Nike 6.0. -*

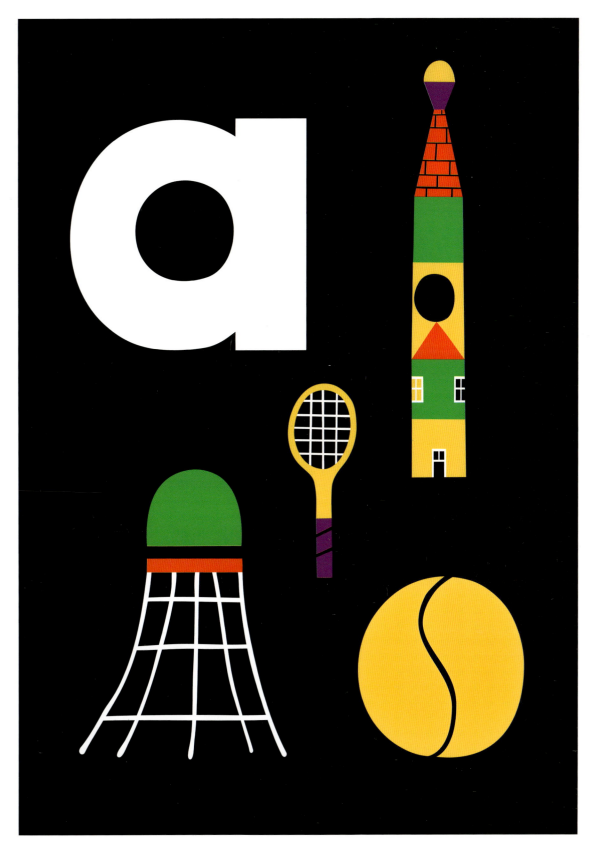

//Andreas Samuelsson// *Untitled. Adidas.* -

114

//Dan Stiles// *LP cover. Sola Rosa. 2009*

//**Dan Stiles**// *CD cover. Folk Music compilation, Universal Music Group. 2009*

//Dan Stiles// *Untitled. Sigur Rós poster. 2006*

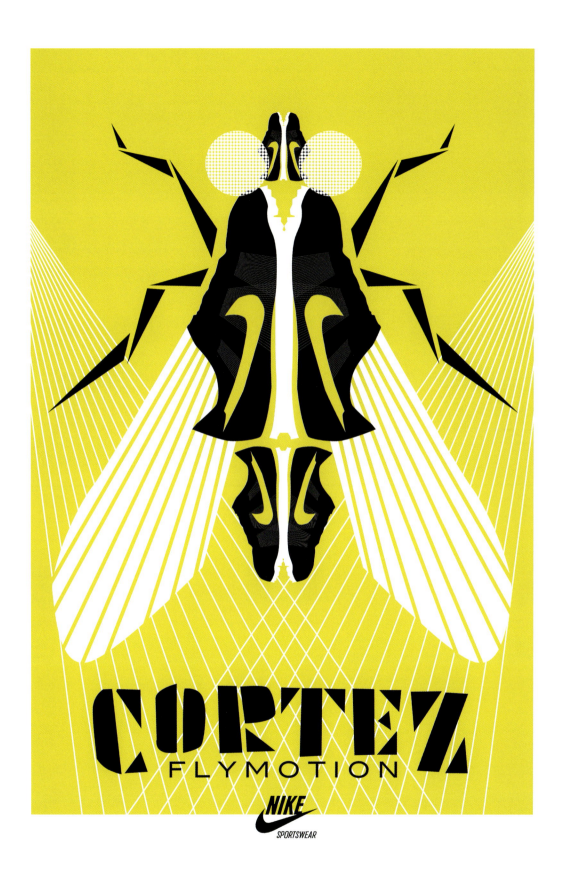

//Dan Stiles// *Cortez Poster. Nike. 2008*

SHOWBOX SEATTLE
SCISSOR SISTERS
OCTOBER 2&3

//Dan Stiles// *Scissor Sisters. Showbox Seattle. 2006*

//**Dan Stiles**// *Major Lazer. Roseland Theater. 2010*

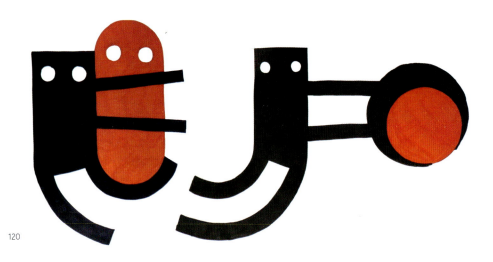

réutilisables

//Fabricio Caiazza (Faca)// *Untitled. Personal work. 2007*

//Fabricio Caiazza (Faca)// *Untitled. Personal work. 2007*

//Fabricio Caiazza (Faca)// *Untitled. Personal work. 2010*

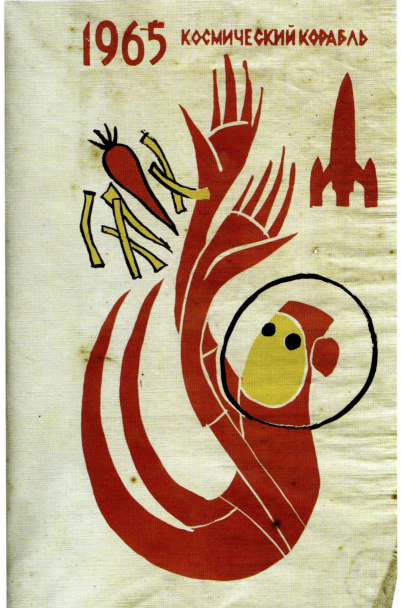

//Fabricio Caiazza (Faca)// *Untitled. Personal work. 2010*

TO THE FOREST

CAMPING ZONE

TO THE TOILETS

//Javier Arce// *Camping. Raak Magazine. 2010*

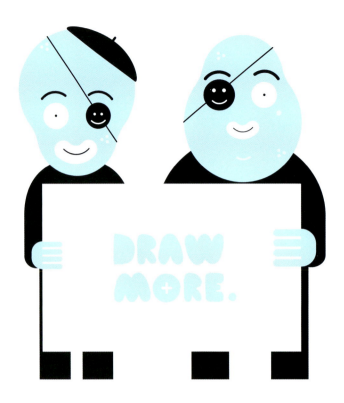

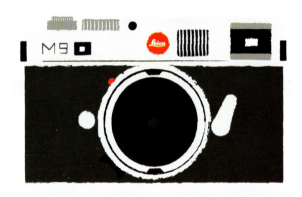

//Javier Arce// *Draw More. Personal work. 2010*
//Javier Arce// *My Leica. Personal work. 2010*

//**Javier Arce**// *Lucky Caco. Personal work. 2010*

//Javier Arce// *Untitled. Personal work. 2010*
//Javier Arce// *Surrealist Cards. 452° F . 2010*

//**Javier Arce**// *La Pera. Personal work. 2010*

//**Kari Modén**// *Untitled. Tvardrag magazine. 2010*
//**Kari Modén**// *Untitled. Active Internacional. 2010*

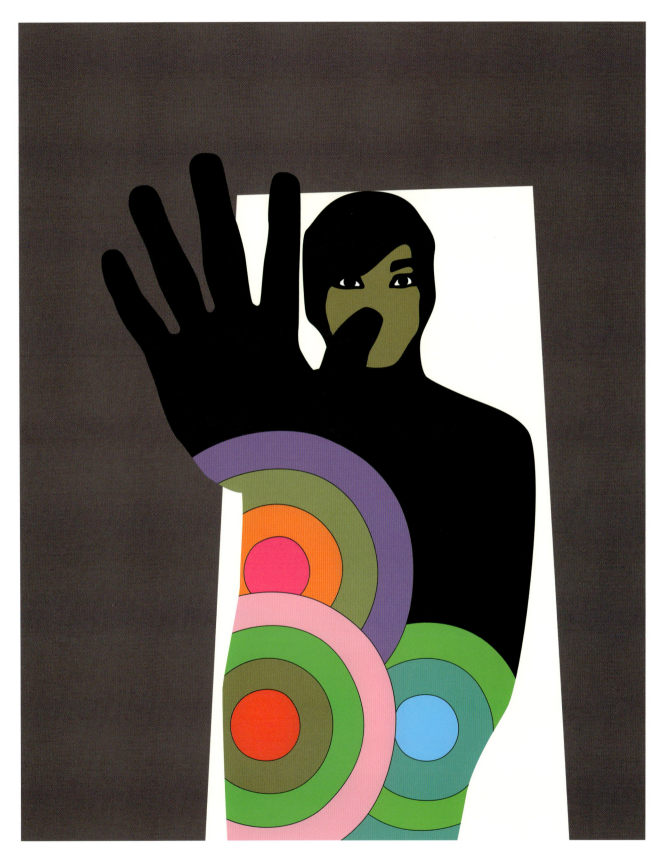

//**Kari Modén**// *Untitled. Tvardrag magazine. 2010*

//Kari Modén// *Walk Tall. T-shirt Gap. 2008*

//**Kari Modén**// *Untitled. Inspire magazine. 2010*

//Kari Modén// *Na No. Tvardrag magazine. 2010*

//Kari Modén// *Untitled. Kupé magazine. 2010*

FRUIT SALAD

//**Max Estes**// *Oslo Neighborhood. Forthcoming Children's Book. 2009*

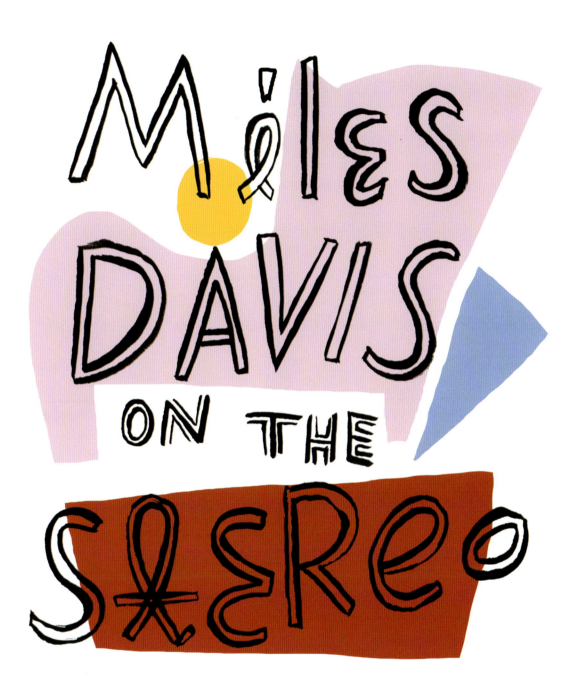

//**Max Estes**// *Miles. Personal work. 2009*

//**Max Estes**// *Let's Roll. Forthcoming Children's Book. 2010*
//**Max Estes**// *Enjoy Autumn. Forthcoming Children's Book. 2010*

//**Max Estes**// *Lipstick. Personal work. 2009*
//**Max Estes**// *Spindle Head. Forthcoming Children's Book. 2010*

//**Max Estes**// *Language. Personal work. 2009*

//**Max Estes**// *Messy. Personal work. 2009*

ka ka ka ka ka ka ka ka ka ka ka ka

ka ka ka k ka ka ka ka ka ka

kilo kimono kimono kimono

kilo kilo kilo kilo kilo kilo

kábila kabila kabila

kabila kabila kabila

kimono kim

kimono kimono kim

Hacer que los niños coloreen los dibujos del cuaderno es contribuir en gran medida al desarrollo del sentido es

//Marc Taeger// *Sketchbook. Richard Brereton. -*

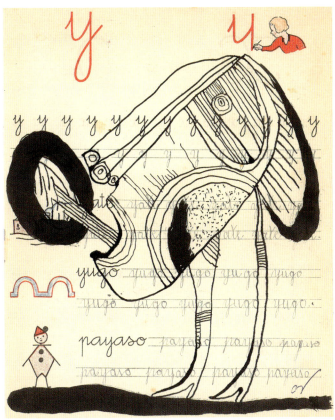

//**Marc Taeger**// *Sketchbook. Richard Brereton.* -
//**Marc Taeger**// *Sketchbook. Richard Brereton.* -
//**Marc Taeger**// *Garbancito. Kalandraka Editions.* -

146

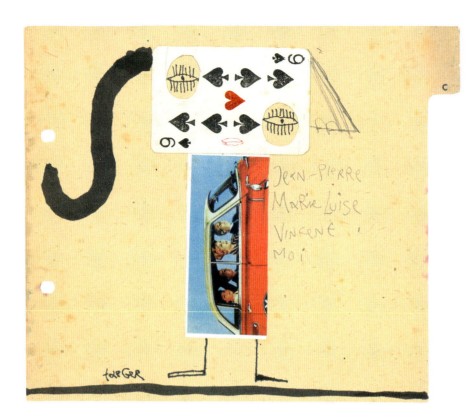

//**Marc Taeger**// *Jean Pierre. Laurence King Publishing.* -
//**Marc Taeger**// *Caballo. Laurence King Publishing.* -

//**Marc Taeger**// *Taimtogo. Laurence King Publishing.* -

//**Mikel Jaso**// *La peligrosa tecnología nuclear. Público newspaper. 2008 /* G-8, sin novedades. *Público newspaper. 2009*
Los salarios de España. *Público newspaper. 2010 / Truth of dare. New York Times. 2010*

//**Mikel Jaso**// *Viva Marx, viva el capital. Público newspaper. 2008*

//**Mikel Jaso**// *The Influencers. Lo peor de cada casa. Público newspaper. 2008*

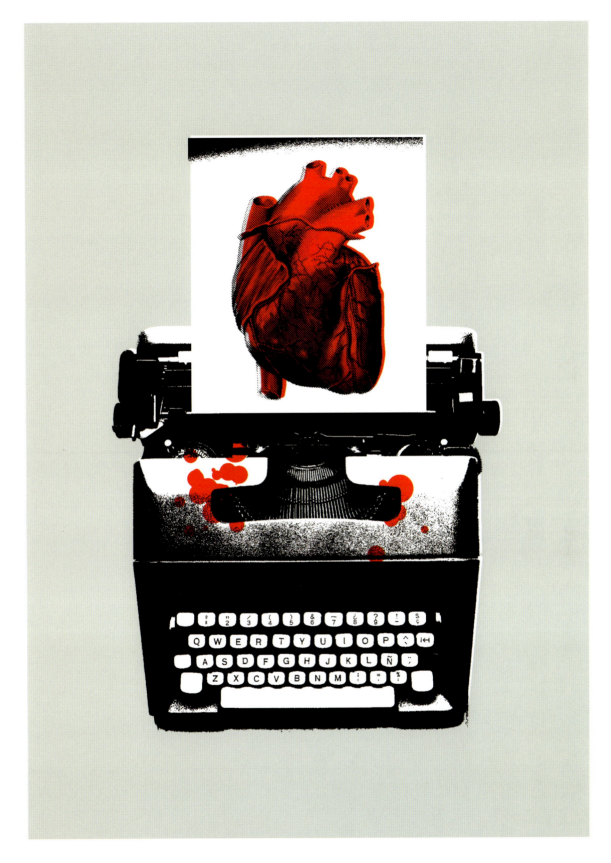

//**Mikel Jaso**// *Vida perra. La literatura sólo vive de fantasía. Público newspaper. 2008*

//**Mikel Jaso**// *Esperpento hispánico. Público newspaper. 2008*

//**Mikel Jaso**// *Untitled. Personal work. 2009*

//**Nazario Graziano**// *All is full of love. Personal work. -*

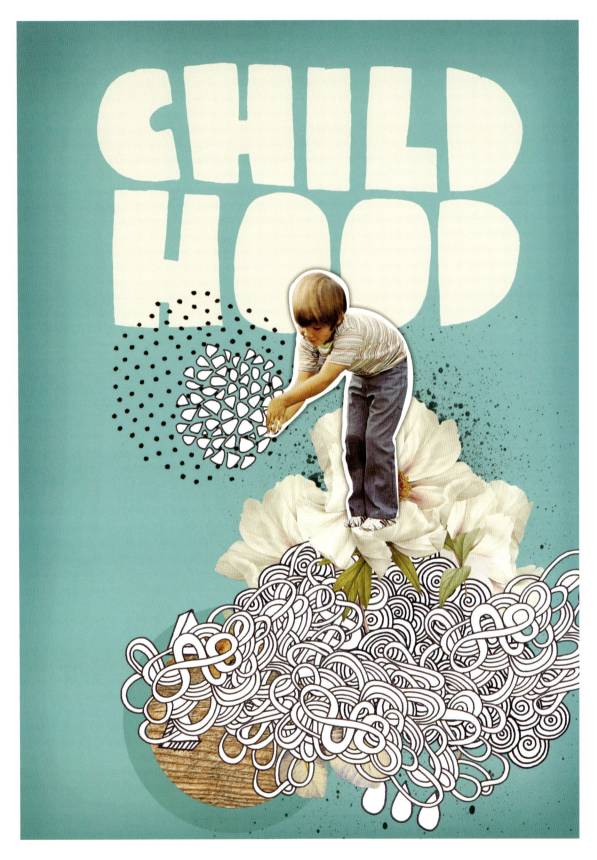

//Nazario Graziano// *Childhood. Personal work.* -

//**Nazario Graziano**// *Untitled. Milk magazine.* -

//Nazario Graziano// *Untitled. Super 8 magazine. -*

//**Blanca Gómez**// *My pencil pot. Personal work. 2009*
//**Blanca Gómez**// *Bakers Dozen. Bakers Dozen Shop. 2009*

//Blanca Gómez// *Bonjour. Personal work. 2009*

//Blanca Gómez// *Monsieur. Personal work. 2008*

//Blanca Gómez// *Let's Play. The Art Group. 2009*

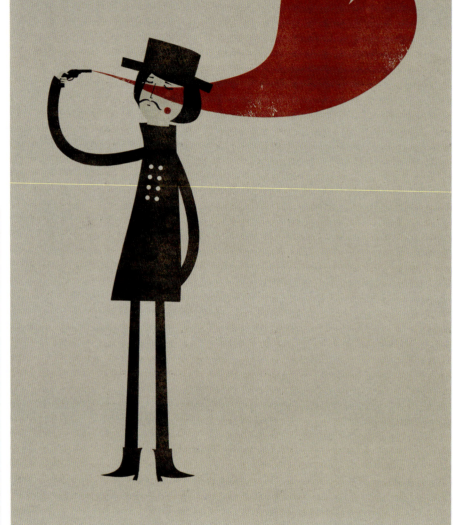

//Blanca Gómez// *Rainynight. Personal work. 2009*
//Blanca Gómez// *Pum. Cabaret poster. 2009*

//Blanca Gómez// *The Writer. Personal work. 2008*

//Bombo// *Miami. Miami Milan Festival. 2009*

//Bombo// *Retour. Bayard Jeunesse France. 2010*

//Bombo// *Le Secret. Bayard Jeunesse France. 2010*

//**Bombo**// *Reves. Bayard Jeunesse France. 2010*

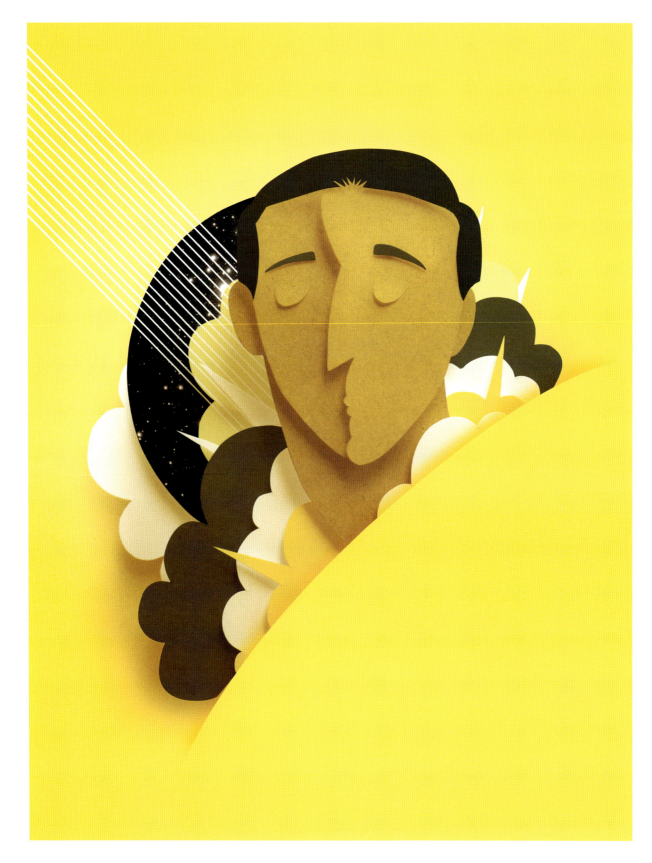

//Bombo// *Shiala Beouf. Nick magazine Italy. 2009*

//Bombo// *Vecinos. Atypica magazine. 2008*
//Bombo// *Neighbours. D-Home magazine. 2009*

FIND OUT
WHAT
THE FUTURE
HOLDS IN
STORE
FOR YOU

RANJIT
SINGH

//Martin Haake// *Ranjit singh. Personal work for Illustrative. 2009*

//Martin Haake// *Food. Essentesten. -*

//**Martin Haake**// *General. 3x3 magazine.* -

//**Martin Haake**// *Family. Exhibition at Johanssen gallery Berlin.* -

//Martin Haake// *Brick Layer. Building magazine. -*
//Martin Haake// *People. Personal work. -*
//Martin Haake// *Weird rules. Personal work. -*

//Martin Haake// *Untitled. Dogs magazine.* -

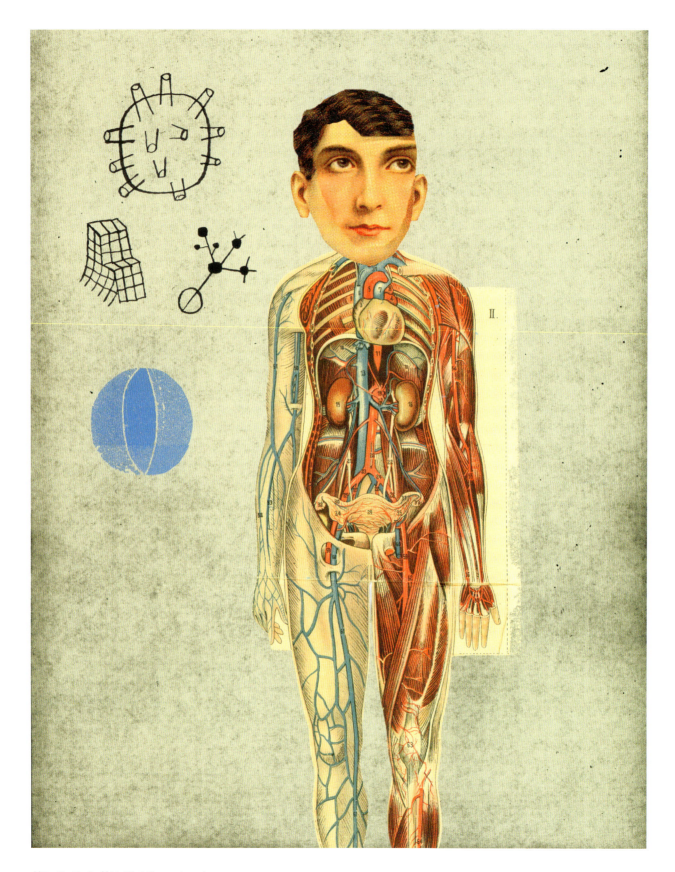

//Martin Haake// *Untitled. Personal work.* -

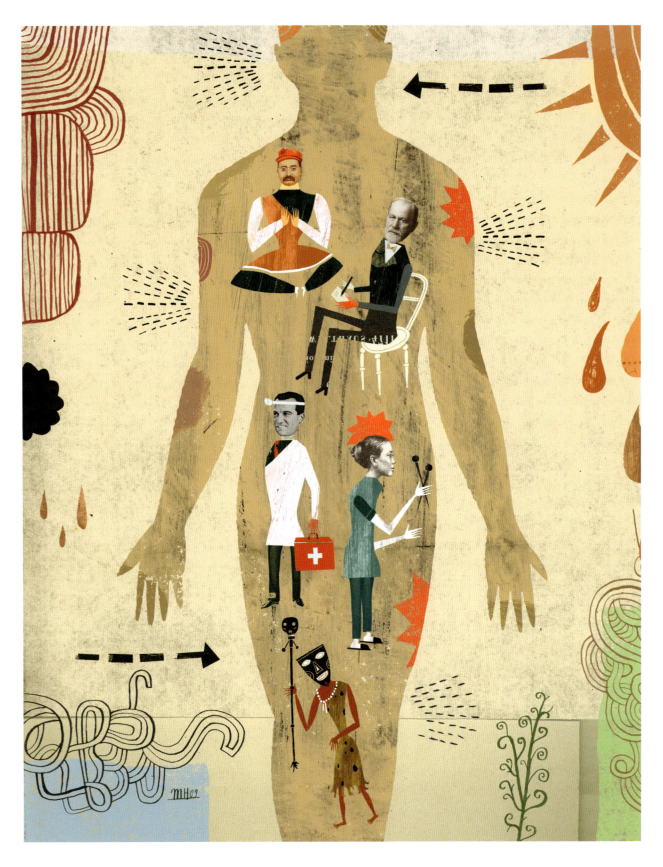

//Martin Haake// *Untitled. Myself magazine.* -

180

//Simon Peplow// *Necessary Pursuits. Carhartt Streetwear.* -

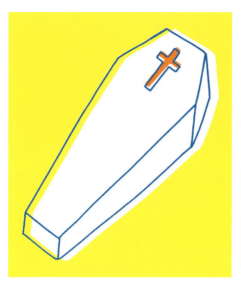

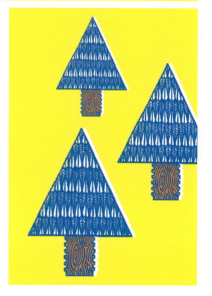

//Simon Peplow// *You find a way of keeping. Mouth magazine. -*

//Simon Peplow// *Its not what you say... well yes it is!. Memphis magazine.* -

//Simon Peplow// *Cradle. Giant Robot New York.* -

//Simon Peplow// *The Visitor. LeBook London-Paris.* -

//Simon Peplow// *Creative Block. Giant Robot New York. -*

//**Daniel Sesé**// *La detección de la violencia de parejas hacia mujeres. Doyma Editions. -*
//**Daniel Sesé**// *Motivación en las organizaciones. Jano magazine. -*

//Daniel Sesé// *Sacar a África del agujero. Press illustration.* -

//Daniel Sesé// *Language book. SM Editions. -*

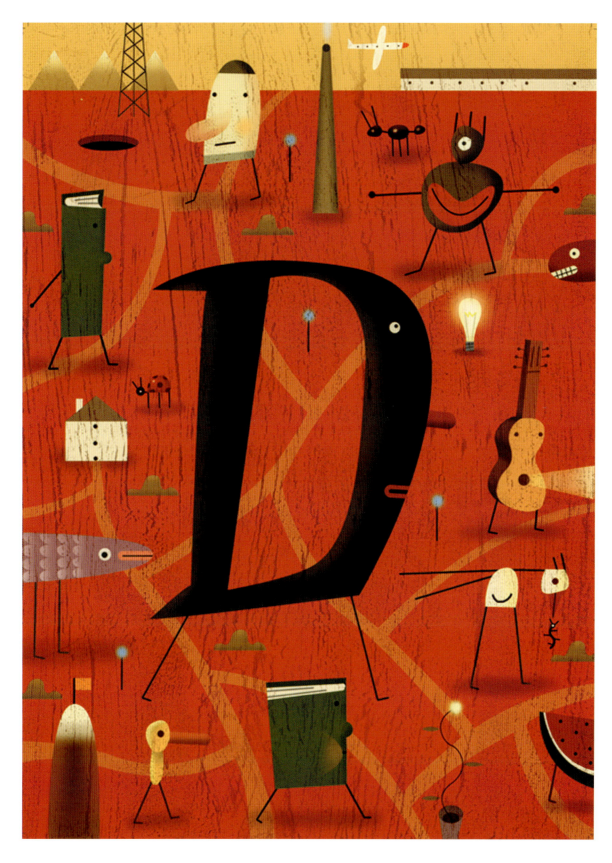

//**Daniel Sesé**// *Letra D, project Educamos. Grupo SM. -*

//Daniel Sesé// *Hi havia una vegada... .Cruïlla. -*

//**Daniel Sesé**// *Es momento de reflexionar. Jano magazine.* -

//Sac Magique// *Untitled. Plastique magazine. 2009*
//Sac Magique// *Chinese repair. Image magazine. 2009*

//Sac Magique// *Kasms. PlanB magazine. 2009*

194

//Sac Magique// *Untitled. Woo Agentur. 2009*

//Sac Magique// *Untitled. Woo Agentur. 2009*

196

//Sac Magique// *Ice Cream Wars. Personal work. 2009*
//Sac Magique// *Croc. Ink Departament Store. 2009*
//Sac Magique// *Emmy the Great. PlanB magazine. 2009*

//Sac Magique// *Untitled. Cono Sur. 2009*

//**Mikel Casal**// *San Francisco. ABC newspaper. 2009*

//Mikel Casal// *Siesta. ABC newspaper. 2009*

//Mikel Casal// *Cantantes. ABC newspaper. 2009*

//Mikel Casal// *Ella. Público newspaper. 2009*

//**Mikel Casal**// *Coyoacan. ABC newspaper. 2010*

//**Mikel Casal**// *Solar. Público newspaper. 2009*

//**Mikel Casal**// *Vineyard. ABC newspaper. 2010*

///Mikel Casal// *Energía. El Correo newspaper. 2010*

//Cristóbal Schmal// *Juedisch, Jüdishe allgemeine, Berlin. 2009*

//Cristóbal Schmal// *Untitled, Walk In magazine, Barcelona. 2009*

//Cristóbal Schmal// *Lars von Trier, Kate Moss, Paris Hilton.*
Martini Book, Russia. 2010

//Cristóbal Schmal// *Seit, Jüdishe allgemeine, Berlin. 2009*

//**Cristóbal Schmal**// *Lit_s, Jüdishe allgemeine, Berlin. 2009*

//**Cristóbal Schmal**// *Liebe, Jüdishe allgemeine, Berlin. 2009*

//David Pohl// *Blood and Tears. Minnesota Monthly. 2006*

//David Pohl// *Sinking Economy. The Miami Herald. 2008*

//**David Pohl**// *Neverland. Personal work. 2004*
//**David Pohl**// *Swimming. Personal work. 2004*

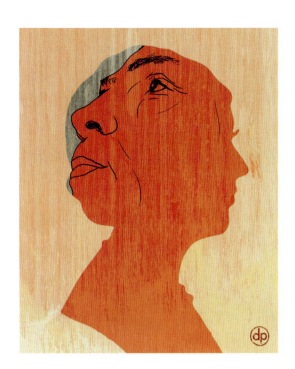

//**David Pohl**// *Memory. Personal work. 2003*
//**David Pohl**// *Drinking and smoking. The New York Times. 2007*

216

HANGOVER?

GOOD LUCK!

AFTER YOU INGEST ALCOHOL, YOUR BODY BREAKS IT DOWN INTO (AMONG OTHER THINGS) ACETALDEHYDE, BEFORE CONVER-
TING IT INTO LESS HARMFUL SUBSTANCES. THE ACETALDEHYDE MESSES WITH YOUR BRAIN AT THE SAME TIME AS A HOST OF
DEPLETED MINERALS ARE SHORT-CIRCUITING YOUR NERVOUS SYSTEM, AND THAT'S IN ADDITION TO LOW BLOOD SUGAR AND
THE CLASSIC HEADACHE-AND-DRY-MOUTH SYMPTOMS CAUSED BY DEHYDRATION. THE RESULT: NAUSEA, TWITCHY NERVES,
UNPLEASANTNESS, PESSIMISM, TERRIBLE BRAIN PAIN, AND A TEMPORARY SUSPENSION OF THE LAWS OF GRAVITY.

//Laszlito Kovacs// *Hangover?. Poster, Media Advanced. -*

//Laszlito Kovacs// *Yellow eyer. Personal work. -*

THE
GENTELMAN BROS.
LOVE BUREAU

//**Laszlito Kovacs**// *The Gentleman Bros. Love Bureau. -*
//**Laszlito Kovacs**// *Whale. Poster, Media Advanced. -*
//**Laszlito Kovacs**// *Untitled. Gijón film festival. -*

//Fábrica de Detergentes// *Homo homini lupus. Personal work. 2010*

//**Fábrica de Detergentes**// *Martians. Personal work. 2010*
//**Fábrica de Detergentes**// *Los enfermos. Personal work. 2010*

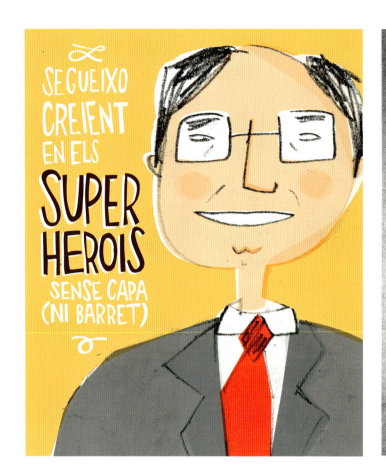

//**Fábrica de Detergentes**// *Segueixo creient en els superherois (sense capa ni barret). PSC. 2010*
//**Fábrica de Detergentes**// *Facebook. Visual magazine. 2010*
//**Fábrica de Detergentes**// *For a walk. Herraizsoto&co - Camper friends. 2010*

//**Fábrica de Detergentes**// *Rainy day. Herraizsoto&co - Camper friends. 2010*

//**Calef Brown**// *Portrait of Jimmy Carl Black. Cut to the Drummer. 2008*
//**Calef Brown**// *Freedom of Speech. Personal work. -*

//Calef Brown// *The King of the Tire, book "Flamingos on the Roof ". Houghton Mifflin Ed. 2006*

//**Calef Brown**// *Benjamin's Toys. The Curious Case of Benjamin Button.*
Harper Collins. 2008
//**Calef Brown**// *Owlentine's Day. Personal work. 2010*
//**Calef Brown**// *Dog's Revenge. Exquisite Corpse Book. 2010*

//Calef Brown// *Soggy Circus. Book "Flamingos on the Roof " . Houghton Mifflin Ed. 2006*

//Iván Bravo// *Mural. Innuo agency. 2010*

//Iván Bravo// *Saxo Jazz. Personal work. 2008*

232

//**Iván Bravo**// *Objetivo del Milenio. Cover InfoASF magazine. 2008*

//**Iván Bravo**// *Bioética. Compartir magazine. 2009*
//**Iván Bravo**// *Educación y esfuerzo. Relleu magazine. 2009*
//**Iván Bravo**// *Zapatos andarines. Personal work. 2008*

BROWNiE

//Stefan Glerum// *Avalanches. DJ Broadcast's Recover Project.* -

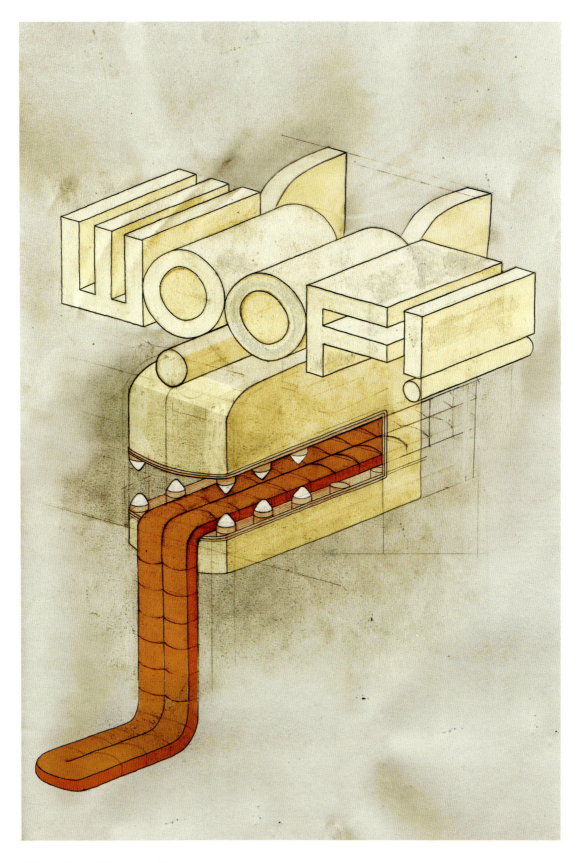

//Stefan Glerum// *Woof. Rozen Theater Amsterdam. -*

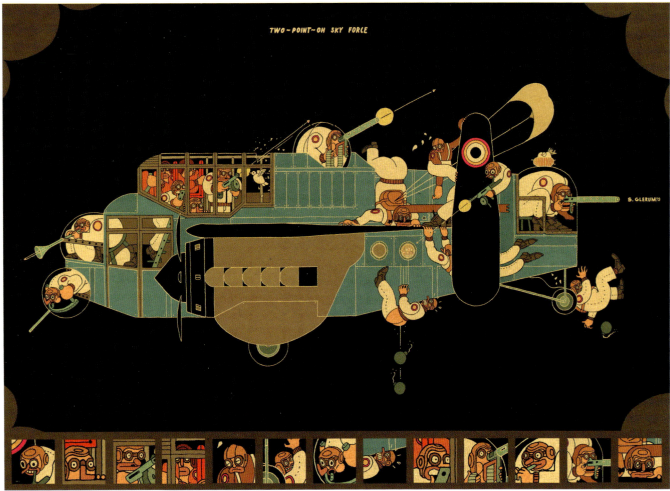

//Stefan Glerum// *Rednose Distrikt. Rednose Distrikt. -*
//Stefan Glerum// *Two-Point-oh Sky Force. Adobe User Group. -*

239

//Stefan Glerum// *Sugar Protocol. New Cool Collective. -*

//**Pantero Pinco**// *O português que se correspondeu com Darwin de Paulo Renato. Cal&Gráfica Editions. -*
//**Pantero Pinco**// *Vacas Flacas. Pocas Páginas Editions. -*

//Pantero Pinco// *Geezuz. Personal work. -*

//Pantero Pinco// *Cabeza de monete. Personal work.* -

//Pantero Pinco// *Le quedan 3 para septiembre. Personal work. -*

club de creativos.
calle de la palma 11,
28004 madrid.
www.clubdecreativos.com

c de c barcelona
comercio, 64, 2 ~ 1
08003 barcelona

//Oscar Llorens// *Untitled. CdC, Club de Creativos. 2008*

//Oscar Llorens// *11S. Personal work. 2006*

//Oscar Llorens// *Universo. Personal work. 2008*

//Oscar Llorens// *Untitled. Visual magazine. 2008*

//Luis Urculo// *Encyclopedia. Personal work. 2009*

//**Luis Urculo**// *Alfombras residuales. Casa Encendida, Madrid. 2009*

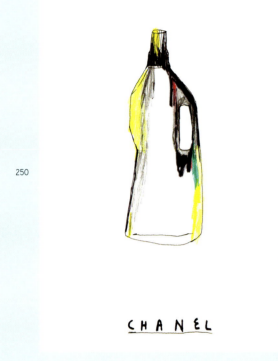

CHANEL

GUCCI

DIOR
DIOR
DIOR

//Luis Urculo// *Clean series. Personal work. 2008*

//Luis Urculo// *Airon Maiden. Personal work. 2007*

//Fernando Elvira// *Liburuak. Algatocín. 2009*

//Fernando Elvira// *S.A. Airon Estudio de Sonido. 2008*

//Fernando Elvira// *Rosa version. Personal work. 2009*

//**Fernando Elvira**// *10 Mimbres. Algotacín. 2009*
//**Fernando Elvira**// *X-ray series. Algotacín. 2009*

//**Fernando Elvira**// *Irak Personal work. Las Arenas. 2003*
//**Fernando Elvira**// *Txirrindula. Algotacín. 2009*

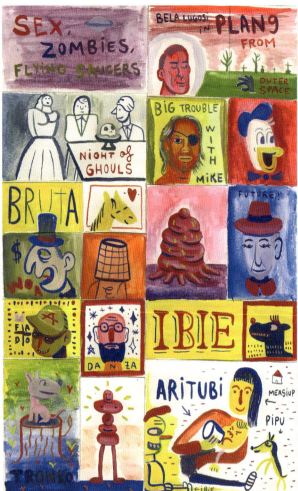

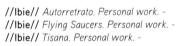

//**Ibie**// *Autorretrato. Personal work.* -
//**Ibie**// *Flying Saucers. Personal work.* -
//**Ibie**// *Tisana. Personal work.* -

257

//Ibie// *Machete. Personal work.* -

//Ibie// *Brutopy. Personal work.* -
//Ibie// *Kaiman. Personal work.* -

//lbie// *Lagoon y Mersiup. Personal work.* -

//**Jack Teagle**// *The Fight. Personal work. 2009*

//Jack Teagle// *Heroes and Villains. Personal work. 2009*

//Jack Teagle// *Total Alienation. Personal work. 2010*

//Jack Teagle// *Reading consumers' minds. Research World Magazine. 2009*

//Jack Teagle// *Spera. Spera Comics. 2009*

//Jack Teagle// *Happy. YCN Group. 2010*

//Jack Teagle// *True Tales. Personal work. 2009*

//Jack Teagle// *Elvis Lives. Personal work. 2009*

CONTRIBUTORS

270

271

RETINA & RETINETTE

Nous Retina et Retinette

// Le monde a besoin de banquiers et de fonction-naires, mais nous ne sommes pas le monde. Nous sommes nous-mêmes et nous habitons notre écosystème particulier, empreint de couleurs et de cabanes en bois. Nous sommes designers & lovers et nous vivons à Barcelone (suivant les conseils de nos avocats, nous ne feront aucun commentaire sur cette ville). Nous aimons rire, marcher au soleil et faire des figurines en pain d'épice, entre autres choses.

En peu de mots, nous aimons nous amuser. Et nous voulons transmettre cette joie de vivre à tra-vers les couleurs et les formes. Car nous aimons l'illustration et nous donnerions presque tout pour elle. Ainsi nous allons en faire le tour au sein de ce livre intitulé *Picnic* et nous aimerions que tous ceux possédant la main et le cerveau hyperactifs, comme nous, se rassasient de beauté.

C'est pour cela que nous continuerons toujours à porter dans notre sac des armes de destruction massive : des stylos et des cahiers. Parce que même si ces messieurs vêtus de costumes en tergal insistent pour faire de ce monde un lieu de répliques insipides, nous n'allons pas céder. Nous irons en pique-nique avec tous ceux qui veulent se joindre à nous et continuer à sauver les écureuils et autres espèces protégées.

Bonne digestion

Somos Retina y Retinette

// El mundo necesita banqueros y funciona-rios, pero nosotros no somos el mundo. Somos nosotros mismos y habitamos nuestro particular ecosistema, lleno de colores y casitas de madera. Somos designers & lovers y vivimos en Barcelona (siguiendo los consejos de nuestros abogados, no vamos a opinar sobre esta ciudad). Nos gusta reírnos, pasear al sol y hacer galletas de muñecos, entre otras cosas.

Nos gusta divertirnos en un verbo-palabra. Y queremos transmitir ese saber vivir a través del color y las formas. Porque amamos la ilustración y lo daríamos casi todo por ella. Por eso la vamos a sacar a pasear en este libro que se llama *Picnic* y nos gustaría que todos los que tienen la mano y el cerebro hiperactivos como nosotros se atraquen de belleza.

Por eso seguimos llevando siempre en el bolso armas de destrucción masiva: bolis y libretas. Por-que aunque los señores de traje de tergal insistan en hacer de este mundo un lugar fotocopiado y aburrido, nosotros no vamos a pasar por el aro. Nos iremos de picnic con todos los que quieran acompañarnos y seguir salvando ardillas y otras especies protegidas.

Feliz digestión

Our names are Retina and Retinette

// The world needs bankers and bureaucrats, but we aren't the world. We are just ourselves, living in our own particular ecosystem, full of colours and wooden houses. We are designers & lovers, and we live in Barcelona (following the advice of our lawyers, that's all we can say about the city). We like laughing, walking in the sun and making gingerbread men (amongst other things).

In a nutshell, we like enjoying ourselves. And we want to get this joie de vivre across in colour and forms. Because we love illustration and would do almost anything for it. That's why we've let it off the leash in this book, which we've called *Picnic*, so that all those people with hyperactive hands and minds, like us, can enjoy this binge of beauty. And so we're not about to stop carrying around weapons of mass destruction –pens and note-books – in our bags. Because however much the men in polyester suits try to make this world a boring place, a replica, we refuse to start jumping through hoops. Instead, we'll be out Picnicking with anyone who wants to come with us, saving squirrels and other endangered species.

Happy digestion

promopress

411851